Gourd Crafts

6 Projects & Patterns

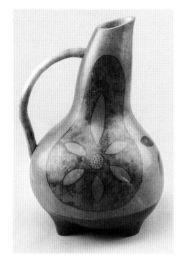

A Handbook of Design Possibilities

Ro Shillingford

Schiffer Publishing Ltd

4880 Lower Valley Road, Atglen, PA 19310

Other Schiffer Books on Related Subjects

Published by Schiffer Publishing Ltd.
4880 Lower Valley Road
Atglen, PA 19310
Phone: (610) 593-1777; Fax: (610) 593-2002
E-mail: Info@schifferbooks.com

For the largest selection of fine reference books on this and related subjects,
please visit our web site at **www.schifferbooks.com**
We are always looking for people to write books on new and related subjects. If
you have an idea for a book please contact us at the above address.

This book may be purchased from the publisher.
Include $3.95 for shipping.
Please try your bookstore first.
You may write for a free catalog.

In Europe, Schiffer books are distributed by
Bushwood Books
6 Marksbury Ave.
Kew Gardens
Surrey TW9 4JF England
Phone: 44 (0) 20 8392-8585; Fax: 44 (0) 20 8392-9876
E-mail: info@bushwoodbooks.co.uk
Website: www.bushwoodbooks.co.uk
Free postage in the U.K., Europe; air mail at cost

Copyright © 2008 by Ro Shillingford
Library of Congress Control Number: 2007939719

Designed by Ro Shillingford
Type set in University Roman Bd BT/Zurich BT

ISBN: 978-0-7643-2825-1
Printed in China

Contents

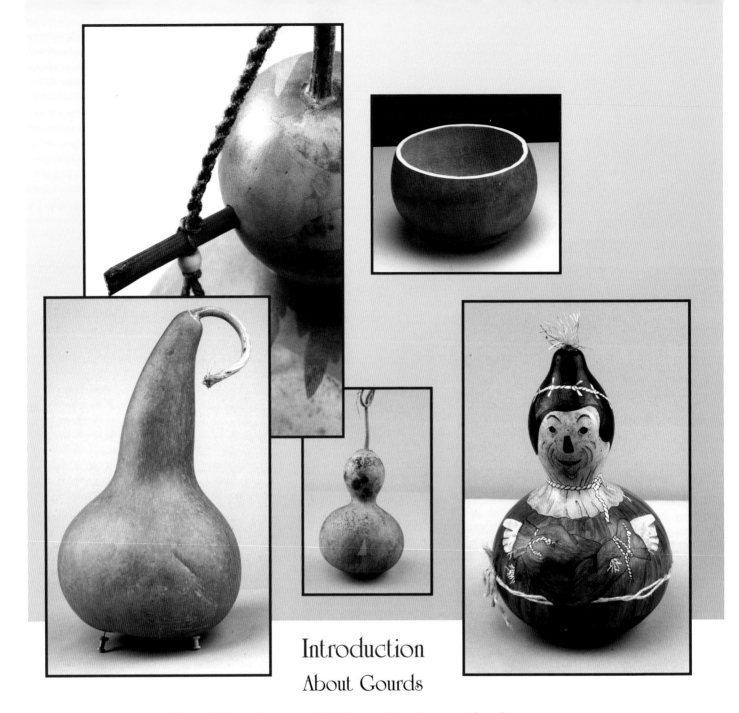

Introduction

About Gourds

Gourds have been used by Humanity wherever they have grown. And why not? Nature has provided a perfect water bottle or storage container or bowl, or even musical instrument, requiring a minimum of effort to make it serviceable. But man did not stop there. Embellished with beads or burning or a bit of carving, the humble gourd is not only useful but a thing of beauty as well. With tools no more complex than a bit of sharpened steel, carvings of fabulous intricacy may be produced; a charred stick lends subtle shadings.

Hard-shell gourds of the genus *Lagenaria* are the ones generally used in craft work. Their green fruits, when matured and cured, have a hard exterior resembling wood. Many techniques used in woodcraft may also be used on gourds.

Chapter 1
Types of Gourds

Gourds of the genus *Lagenaria* come in an amazing array of shapes and sizes, from tiny bottle gourds suitable for salt shakers to giants weighing a hundred pounds or more when green. Some of the more available ones include bird bottle, kettle, bushel basket, swan neck, dipper, apple and pear, maranka, tobacco box, cannon ball, and penguin. The Internet is a great source for obtaining gourds from home growers or there may be a gourd society in your state that can direct you to a local source. If you have the room and a suitably long growing season you can even grow your own. Here in Zone 6 they seem to do fine, and with a little help they can be grown in colder areas as well.

Growing Gourds

Gourds are members of the family *Cucurbitacaea*, and like their cousins, pumpkins and squash, produce long vines with tendrils. The larger members of the group can become quite enormous; therefore, space is essential for growing even one vine. Some varieties benefit from trellising, such as dipper gourds, whose handles won't be straight unless the fruit is hanging while growing. The fruit are also quite heavy, so strong support is needed. I have found that a small dead tree makes a great ready-made trellis. Other varieties, such as kettles and bushel baskets, have fruit that is so heavy that they must be grown on the ground.

Gourds like a rich soil and enjoy a healthy shovelful of compost or well-rotted manure. They may be started indoors to get a jump on the growing season, but they so dislike being transplanted that they can languish for several weeks after the experience, which completely defeats the purpose. Therefore it is best if starting indoors to plant in a cardboard milk carton or similar container that may be put directly in the ground when the time comes, thus disturbing the roots as little as possible. Once established, the vines make amazing progress, seeming to grow right before your eyes. They need little attention after that other than perhaps directing the vines.

Curing Gourds

As the growing season progresses the fruit will turn from green to buff to brown, if given enough time. It is best to leave the fruit as long as the vine has any life in it. When ready to harvest, cut the fruit off, leaving a couple of inches of vine attached to it. Good air circulation is more important than temperature for curing. They may even be left outside or in the field. The green gourd is over ninety percent water, and as this water leaves the gourd over a period of months some spotting and molding may occur. This is normal, but if the gourd becomes soft it must be discarded. The gourd is ready for use when it becomes very light and the seeds rattle.

This small gourd is cured and ready to be cleaned.

Soak the gourd in a bucket of warm water. It will bob like a cork, so cover it with a wet towel.

Cleaning Gourds

The cured gourd has a thin skin covering its hard shell. This is removed by first soaking the gourd or leaving it outside during a rainy spell to soften the skin and then scraping it. If mold is a problem, a little bleach will take care of it.

Scrape with a dull knife.

The clean gourd ready for use.

Scrub off the bits with an abrasive pad.

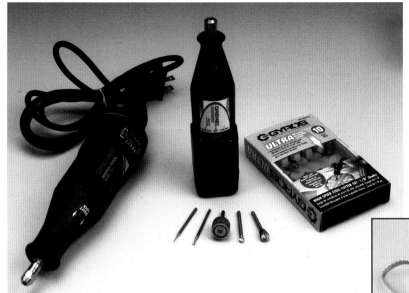

Rotary tools and attachments. Left to right: Variable speed corded Dremel tool; cordless two speed rechargeable Dremel tool; set of ten cutters for rotary tools (they are much more economical to buy this way). In the front: Two small etchers, sanding drum, small and large ball cutters.

Left to right: scraper; clay shaping tool bent at one end; shaped paint scraper; skewer; and kitchen spoon.

Chapter 2
Crafting with Gourds

There are as many ways to decorate a gourd as there are people who do it. Painting, weaving, carving, batiking, burning, cutting, stenciling, all are possibilities, alone or in combination. Once you have mastered some basic skills and the use of the tools, your imagination is your only limitation. So let it go, and most of all, HAVE FUN!

Cutting the Gourd

Hardness of the shell of your particular gourd largely determines the tool necessary to cut it. Gourds vary greatly in this respect. Some varieties, such as bird bottle or apple gourds, usually have shells thin enough to cut with a utility or Exacto™ knife alone. Others, such as the large kettles, are so thick and hard that this method would be extremely frustrating at best. For these, a saw (keyhole or carpenter's) may be used, or a power tool. There are miniature jigsaws made for gourd work that are very useful in that the cut line is very thin, making it excellent for container work or intricate cutouts. Rotary tools, such as the Dremel, also have circular saw blades available, or a carving or etching attachment may be run around the cut line until the cut is through. A little sandpaper can always be used to smooth out your work.

A Word About Rotary Tools

The rotary tool is most valuable in gourd work because of the great variety of attachments available for it. With the proper bit you may carve, sand, and cut your gourd with ease. It is most important when selecting your tool to choose one with variable speeds. A steel carver in the rotary tool burns the gourd easily. While this is not fatal to the gourd, it is fatal to the steel. Heating dulls the cutting edge, which makes the bit run hotter, which dulls it even more . . . pretty soon you are throwing it away. Run the tool at the slowest speed necessary to accomplish the task. And wear a mask! Rotary tools kick up a lot of dust.

Cleaning Out the Gourd

This is a matter of finding or making whatever gets the job done. The selection above seems to fill all my needs. Sanding finishes off the soft lining of the gourd nicely.

Glues

Generally I use Aileen's™ Tacky Glue for its quick grab and flexibility. Occasionally, if waterproof glue is needed for outdoor applications, I will use Duco Cement™. If you are comfortable with a glue gun, this would also be a good choice.

Wood Fillers

There are two types of wood fillers I use. One is solvent-based, such as Plastic Wood. The advantage of this one is its amazing "stick-ability" to the gourd, its durable hardness, and the fact that it accepts paint or stain exactly as the gourd does, that is to say it is pretty resistant. The other type is latex based, such as Elmer's™ carpenter's wood filler. This type is much softer, easier to sand, and more porous than the gourd itself, which makes a stain go dark in that spot. Both types have their uses.

Transferring Drawings

There are times when you will want to draw directly onto the gourd, and other times when you will want to transfer a drawing. Dressmaker's carbon paper is excellent for this. It is readily available, comes in packages of assorted colors, and removes easily with window cleaner. The range of colors from white to dark blue ensures that you will be able to see your line no matter what you are trying to do.

Coloring the Gourd

First it must be stated that gourd walls are water-resistant and very impervious. The first rule is to make sure that the gourd is impeccably clean and then to sand it lightly to help it to accept any surface applications of color. Any medium may be used. Opaque color is achieved by simply painting the surface, but then the natural variations and character of the gourd is lost. Sometimes this is just what you want. At other times some transparency is desired.

Artists oil colors are good for obtaining transparency. They may be rubbed into the surface directly from the tube or mixed with solvent or medium and painted on. Their advantage is their open working time and lovely consistency that allows for great subtlety in the painting. Their disadvantage is the long dry time. Windsor Newton makes a line of alkyd oil colors called Griffon™, which are great because, while they work like conventional oils, they dry much faster.

Acrylic paints in both tube and bottle form (craft paints) may also be used. The craft paint is good for solid color, the tubes for more transparent effects. The use of a medium will give good results when mixed with the tubes for color glazing. Their advantage is the water clean-up and quick dry time (sometimes too quick).

Any product designed for use on wood such as stains, varnishes, and shellac can all be used on gourds. Leather dyes are also very popular for coloring the gourd and yield deep, rich tones. Experimentation and improvisation are called for to discover what works for you and what you like using.

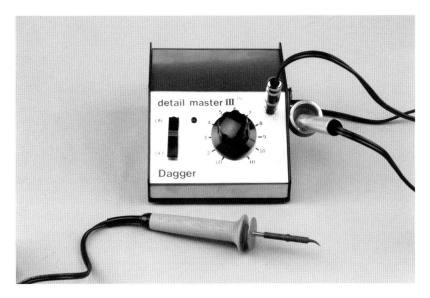

Wood burning tools: The model in the back has variable heat settings and a great variety of available tips. There are even some specifically for gourd work. The little inexpensive unit in the front gives a surprisingly nice line.

Burning

The use of heat imparts a permanent color to the gourd. Wood burning tools can be used to draw and create effects similar to what a pen will do on paper. There are two types of wood burning tools. One type is basically a soldering iron with interchangeable tips. While this type can work, it can be difficult to use because the heat is not controllable and the tendency is to burn the gourd. The other type has a heat control, which allows much more flexibility in the tool.

Due to their individual natures, there is a great range in the amount of heat needed to burn a specific gourd. Practice on a discarded bit if possible.

Another way to use burning is to use a heat source to impart a dark overall color. I have used both a propane torch and a paint stripping heat gun successfully to do this. A gourd with a dark, rich overall tone is known as a "mahogany" gourd.

Carving

Carving involves removing the topmost hard shell of the gourd to expose the softer white part underneath. Carving may be done with small hand tools such as those used for linoleum and wood block work or rotary power tools. Rotary tools are great for this because they work very quickly and there are great ranges of tips available to achieve different results. The exposed white carved area contrasts nicely with the darker gourd wall, or if a dye or stain is applied overall, the opposite effect occurs, as the exposed carved area is more porous than the gourd wall. Both effects can be used to advantage.

Finishing

Any coating used on wood can be used on a gourd, keeping in mind compatibility with whatever substrate or medium is underneath. Spray or brush on, in any degree of shine that complements the work. Wax is also a very traditional and good finish for a gourd. Car wax, neutral shoe polish, and paste furniture wax all work well. Multiple coats will build up a nice sheen.

Chapter 3
Birdhouse

Making a gourd birdhouse is perhaps the most basic thing one can think of to do with a gourd, yet it is very rewarding as the birds seem to love them. The decorating possibilities are vast and with a little care, such as bringing them inside at the end of each season, they will last for many years.

The following chart will help you to create a proper home for the type of bird you wish to attract.

Name of bird	Minimum gourd size in inches	Diameter of entrance hole in inches
wren	4	1
chickadee	4-6	1.25
tufted titmouse	5	1.5
downy woodpecker	5	1.25
nuthatch	5	1.25
bluebird	6-8	1.25
purple martin	6	2.5
flicker	7	2.5

Baby wrens inside their gourd home.

Materials list: Yellow, red, and blue (or green) spray paint, clear or colored plastic adhesive, leaves or templates from the back of this book, stick or dowel, hobby knife, compass.

Determine where you want the hole to be and draw a circle with the compass or a circle template.

Cut open with the knife. Do not attempt to cut all the way through in one pass, make several passes.

Remove the insides with a long handled tool. Here I am using a clay modeling tool.

Mark the bottom for drain holes and drill. Here I have eight holes marked.

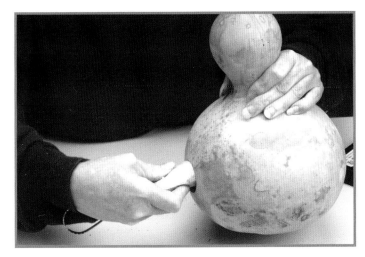

Sand the hole nice and smooth by wrapping sandpaper around a tool handle or dowel.

A stick will be inserted in the top of the gourd for the purpose of hanging. It should be perpendicular to the entrance hole.

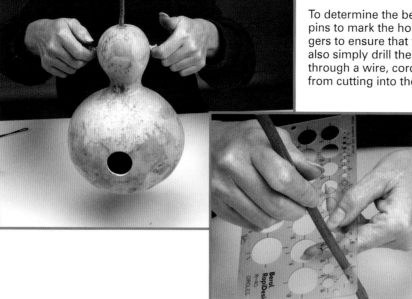

To determine the best placement for the stick, insert push-pins to mark the holes and suspend the pins from your fingers to ensure that the gourd is properly balanced. You could also simply drill the holes and hang the house by threading through a wire, cord or thong. The stick prevents the hanger from cutting into the gourd.

A circle template is handy to determine the size of the stick.

Drill holes: Use a drill bit slightly smaller than the stick. The hole may be reamed out with sandpaper. You want a tight fit.

Insert the stick and trim it to the desired length. Set stick aside. Remove any pencil marks with glass cleaner. The gourd is now ready for decorating.

Trace dry or green leaves onto adhesive paper, or use the leaf shapes provided in the back of this book.

Cut out shapes with scissors or a knife.

Peel and place the leaves randomly on the gourd, creasing as necessary. Don't overlap the leaves at this stage.

Smooth on the leaf. It will be more flexible than the adhesive plastic.

This gourd is ready for spraying.

Alternatively, you can spray an adhesive directly onto a green leaf. Allow it to get a little tacky before applying or it will be difficult to remove.

Spray the yellow first. Make some areas heavy and others quite thin. Let dry.

Next spray the blue. Go easy here and allow areas to mix with the yellow to make greens. Let dry.

13

Peel off the leaves. They may be re-used for the next step or you may use different ones.

Again apply the leaves, this time overlapping where the other ones were to create interesting shapes.

Lastly spray the red SPARINGLY to allow the other colors to show through. Let dry.

Peel off the leaves. The painted leaves look great stuck on the fridge.

The decorating is done. Insert the stick. Any of these materials may be used to make a hanger. Stripped electrical wire is a great source of copper.

For this birdhouse I'm going to make a cord out of a bit of yarn. To make cord, take about three arm's lengths of yarn or string and tie the ends together. Place the tied ends over a hook or doorknob, place a pencil in the loop end, and twirl until the yarn is tightly twisted.

Grab it by the middle and bring the ends together. The yarn will twist up on itself. Smooth it out. It is amazingly resistant to unraveling.

A few knots and pony beads and the hanger is done.

Cord is separated around the stick and knotted up tight on both sides.

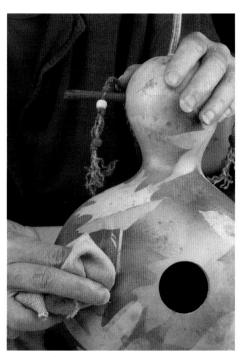

A coat of car wax will protect the birdhouse nicely.

An optional perch may be added. Drill a hole in the same manner as for the hanging stick.

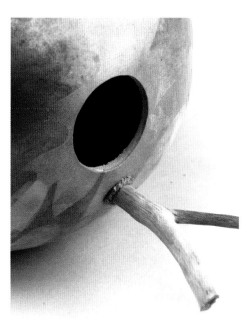

A dab of glue and a wrapping of yarn will hold the perch securely. I used Duco Cement here because it is waterproof.

The finished birdhouse: These make lovely housewarming gifts.

15

Chapter 4
Big Bowl

In this project tape is used to create complex graphics in a simple manner.

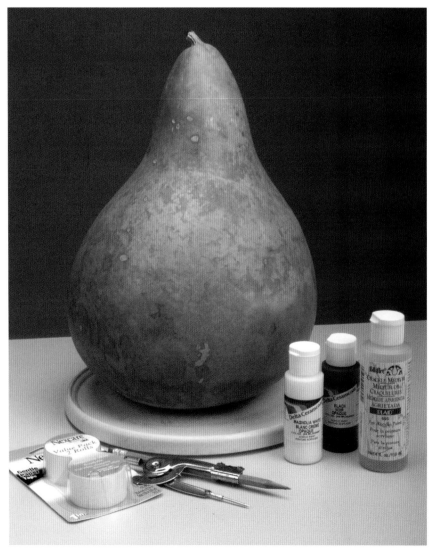

Materials list: Compass, Lazy Susan, flexible tape, black and white water-based craft paint, crackle medium. I am using medical paper tape in one-inch width because it is very flexible and low tack.

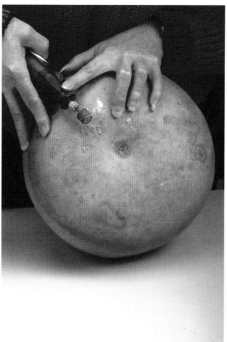

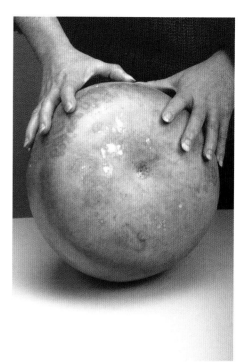

This gourd has some warts and a small hole. It is often the case that an otherwise ideal gourd will have some flaws. First I will fix them.

Fill the hole with Plastic Wood™ and sand off the warts with the sanding drum of the rotary tool. Brace the hand well. Sand off Plastic Wood.

Bottom ready.

Mark the gourd for cutting. Place three small dots of fun tack on the bottom of your gourd.

Place the gourd on the Lazy Susan, spin to center it, and press down.

Mark a cutting line using the compass. Here the compass needs a lift so I am placing the point in the rim of the can to stabilize it. Holding the compass steady, spin the Lazy Susan until you have a complete line.

17

In the same manner, mark down from the cut line 1/4", 3/4", 1-1/2" and 2" for a border.

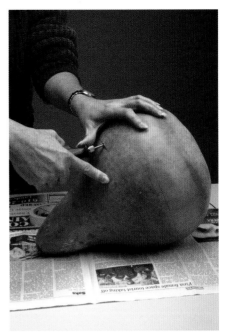

Lift the gourd from the Lazy Susan and remove the fun tack. Cut the gourd. Most large gourds are quite thick and hard and will require a tool such as a keyhole saw, jigsaw or rotary tool to cut them. Here I am using the rotary tool fitted with a small saw blade. Keep the tool perpendicular to the gourd for a flat rim.

Open the gourd, remove the seeds, and scrape clean.

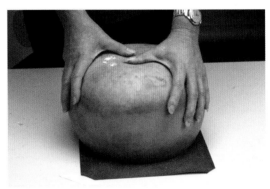

Flatten the rim of the bowl by taping a piece of coarse sandpaper to a flat surface and rubbing it back and forth. Sand the inside until smooth.

Bowl is ready for painting.

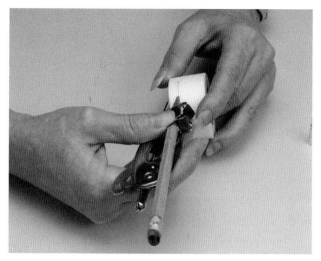

I am going to cut one of the rolls of tape to create two different widths on that roll. Mark the tape at 1/4", then set the compass at the mark and run a line around.

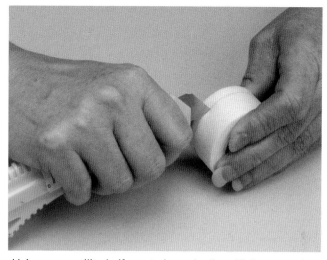

Using your utility knife, cut along the line. Make several passes, going deeper each time.

Tape off the border as shown. Use the 3/4" width in the center section and place a band of tape on each side of the 1/2" sections. Stretch the tape slightly to allow it to lie flat around the curves. With the taping complete, apply black paint in the top and bottom borders. Allow it to dry.

Peel off the center tape.

Place 1/4" strips of tape across the center border on a diagonal. This will become the gourd colored part of the pattern. It is helpful to pre-cut the 1/4" wide strips of tape and place in a handy location.

Apply black paint between each diagonal strip. Let dry.

Remove tape from the center and bottom of the border.

Apply tape over the black border.

Randomly apply 1/4" wide tape, dividing the gourd into interesting shapes. These will become the gourd-colored centers of the stripes.

Paint each area with black. You could paint completely over the tape but leaving the tape unpainted will make the next step easier. Let it dry.

Center a 1" wide strip of tape over each thin strip. Setting your compass at 3/8" and dragging it along the edge of the thin strip will give you a guide line for centering the 1" tape easily.

Apply a thick coat of crackle glaze to the areas between the tape, according to label directions. Do not back brush this product! Let it dry thoroughly.

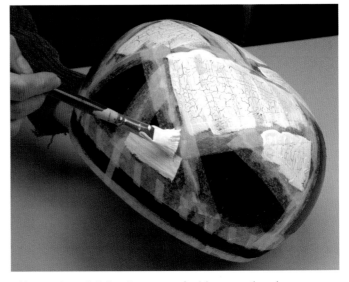

Now paint a full flowing coat of white over the glaze. Again, do not back brush. Crackling will begin immediately and continue until the paint is dry.

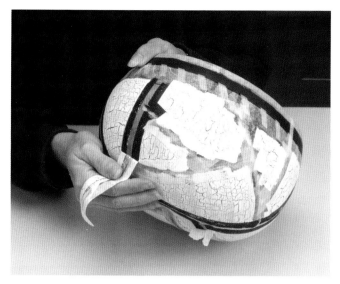

When THOROUGHLY dry, carefully remove the tape.

Peeling the tape back on itself gives a cleaner result.

I decided to add a white bar in the top border. First place tape around the top and bottom of the brown bars.

Then center a piece of tape over each brown bar, covering an equal amount of black on each side. The tape is transparent enough to see through.

Paint the white. Let dry and remove all the tape.

The crackle glaze needs a top coat. Spray or brush on the coating of your choice. Here I am using a Zar™ satin polyurethane because I like the sheen. Inverting the bowl on a large can allows you to coat the whole thing at once.

The inside may be left as is or varnished. I varnished mine.

The finished bowl.

Chapter 5
Big Apple Box

This project introduces carving, using oil paint glazes, and the principles involved in creating a container.

Materials list: Apple gourd, rotary carving tool, red and green artists' oils, oil-based varnish, carbon paper, Lazy Susan, compass.

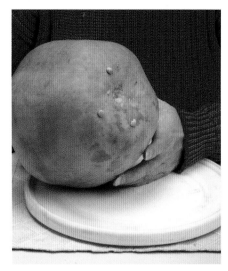

Apply fun tack to the bottom of the gourd and center on the Lazy Susan.

Set the compass well below the shoulder of the gourd, hold the compass steady and spin the Lazy Susan to mark the cut.

Divide the gourd into three sections. Mark a line from the stem to the cut line

Items for transferring.

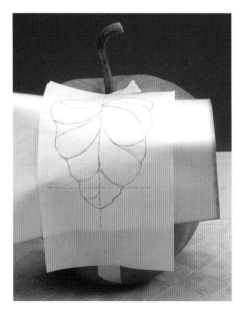

Align center line of the leaf pattern with your marked line and slip the carbon paper under it with the colored side down.

Trace the pattern. Press hard. Repeat for the other two sides.

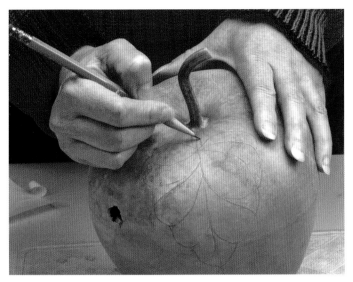

Use the centering line to draw in the stem.

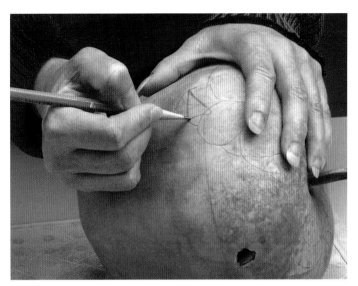

One leaf must be different to create a "key." Redraw the tip of one leaf to fold back onto itself.

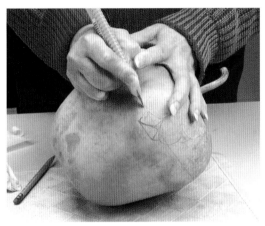

For the top and bottom of any container to fit together properly it is important that the cut itself remove as little material as possible. A mini jig saw sold for gourd work would be a good choice. Fortunately, apple gourds are not very thick; therefore it is possible to cut them with the knife.

Cut along the line and under each leaf tip, making as many passes as needed to cut through.

Open the gourd and remove the seeds. These came out in one piece!

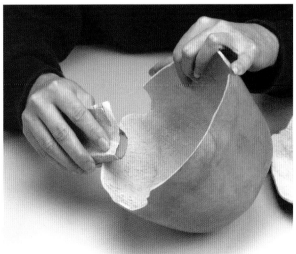

Sand the edge VERY lightly. Do not remove any more material than is absolutely necessary.

25

An eraser makes a good sanding block for flat areas.

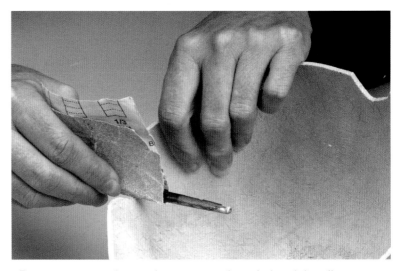

For curves, wrap the sandpaper around a paintbrush handle or dowel.

Fixing a Hole

This gourd has a large hole, but I liked its shape. The hole can be repaired.

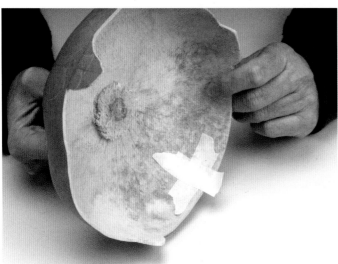

Crisscross two pieces of masking tape on the inside of the gourd over the hole.

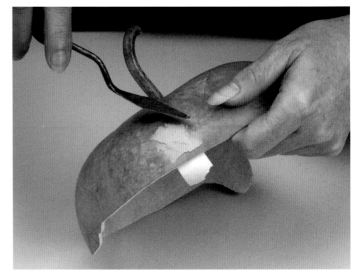

Fill the hole with Plastic Wood and let it dry.

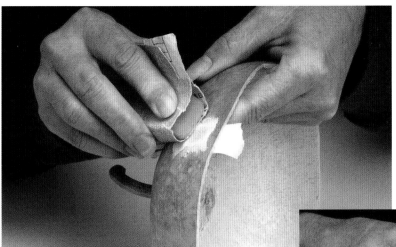

Sand the patch with the sanding block.

Remove the tape.

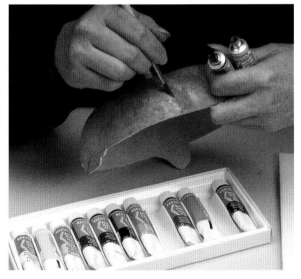

Color the patch with a small amount of yellow ocher and burnt sienna tube acrylics. If your gourd is light, sometimes a little white is needed. You don't need water, just mix the paint right on the gourd.

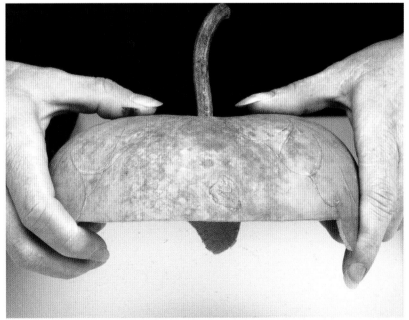

Patch complete.

Place a small amount of green on your palette. A glazed ceramic tile makes a great palette. Here I am using permanent green mixed with Zar™ varnish to create glazes of varying densities. The more varnish, the more olive the color will be.

Paint each section of the leaves. Since the line will be carved it is not necessary to go right up to the line.

Paint the bottom by mixing red with varnish in the same way as the green.

A tall can placed on the Lazy Susan can be used to hold the gourd for painting, spinning as you go around. Mixing directly on the gourd will allow nice natural variations to occur.

Next paint the red on the lid. Allow to dry thoroughly.

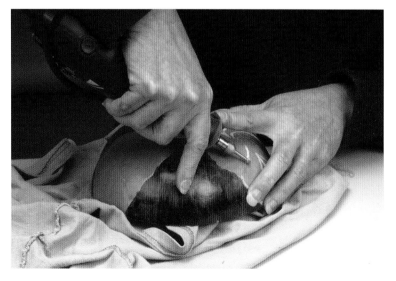

Begin outlining the leaves using the rotary tool with the round ball tip.

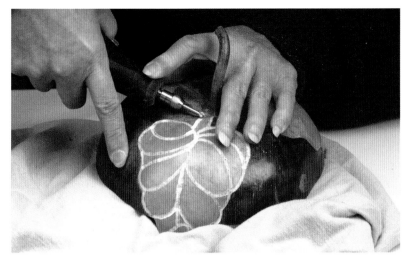

One leaf complete. Complete the other leaves in the same way.

Paint the rim – I'm using a red craft paint here. Running the brush on its side will help prevent slop-overs.

Your container may be personalized. I think I'll make this one for my editor. Lay out your message with chalk.

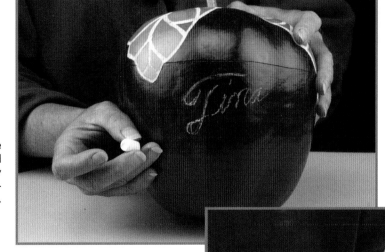

Carve with a small ball tool.

A coat of the varnish will even up the shine. Keep it out of the carvings, though.

Finished box, front.

Finished box, back.

Chapter 6
Inlaid Whimsy-bird Vase

This project explores the creation of a "mahogany" gourd (an all over dark tone achieved by burning), making inlay by the use of wood filler, and the mounting of the gourd on a base for stability.

Techniques for making a mahogany gourd are as ancient and simple as just laying the oiled gourd near an open fire. Other options include the use of a propane torch, or even broiling it in the oven (however, when I tried this one it exploded!). I have here introduced a safer albeit slower method. The object for this project is to produce an overall dark tone for the inlay to show up against. A leather dye would also be a good choice for this.

Materials list: Gourd, paint stripping heat gun, a latex-based wood filler such as Elmer's, rotary tool with small etching bits, saucer or other base, tube oil paints of your choice.

I want a pattern in my burn so I have cut some small shards of contact paper and placed them randomly over the gourd. They will resist the burn.

Oil the gourd in preparation for burning. This helps it to toast evenly. Mineral or cooking oil are both fine. Always burn a gourd BEFORE cutting it!

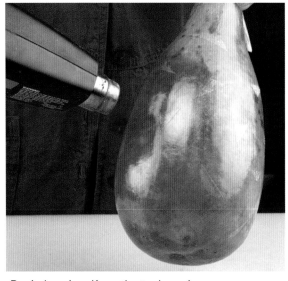

Begin burning. Keep the tool moving.

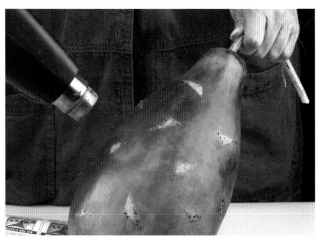

Continue burning until the desired color is achieved. Replenish the oil as needed.

Peel off the shards. Wash the gourd to remove excess oil.

This gourd will be mounted on a little terra cotta plant saucer to add stability and weight. Other options for bases include a scrap of wood or even part of another gourd. The gourd will be cut at the line but I'll leave it for now, as it's easier to work on whole.

Cut your birds and swirls apart and tape in position.

Transfer the design using carbon paper.

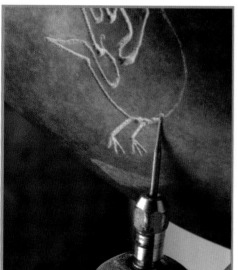

Outline the birds with a tiny etcher.

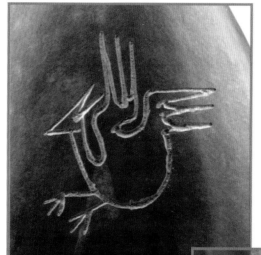

Outline complete.

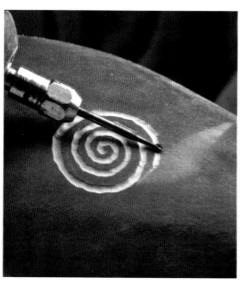

Cut the spirals with a ball tool.

Remove the material inside the bird. A rough cut helps the filler grab.

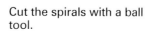

Apply filler onto the birds and spirals.

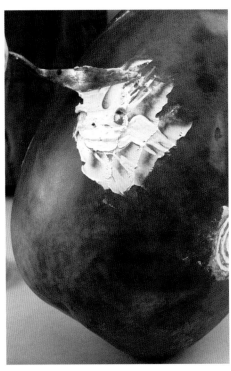

Press it in well.

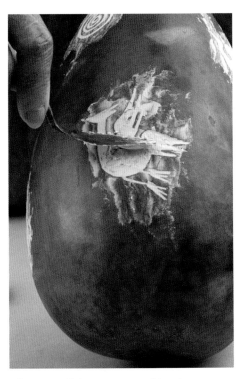

Scrape off the excess and let dry.

The gourd wall is so resistant (and oily) that you can simply wipe off the excess filler by rubbing it with a damp rag.

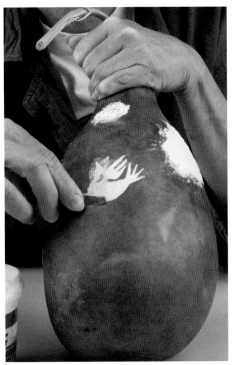

Apply another coat of filler with an eye to filling in any gaps and contouring it to the gourd. Let dry.

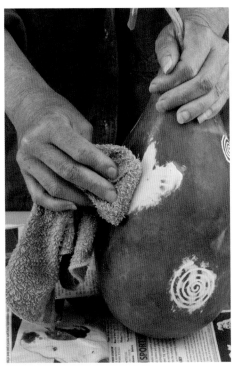

Again wipe with the rag. Even thick patches will come clean.

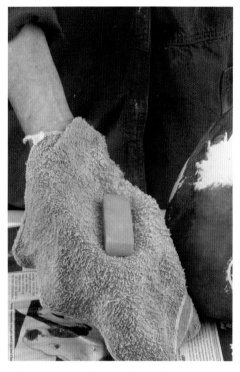

An eraser in the rag keeps the contour of the gourd true.

Wipe it clean.

Fine sandpaper may be used, but be careful not to scarify the gourd wall.

This looks great the way it is, but I think I'll add some color.

Rub some cerulean blue straight from the tube onto the inlay.

Wipe it off. It will stick to the filler but not to the gourd.

Now yellow ocher ...

and orange.

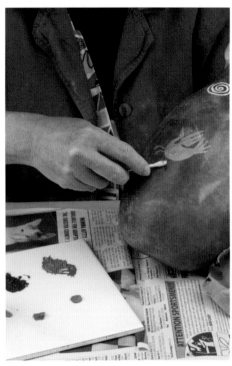

Any excess on the gourd can be easily removed with a swab or brush dipped in solvent. Let all the paint dry thoroughly.

The spiral was colored with a permanent marker.

Time to cut the top off. I don't care if it's level but I do want it straight. This backsaw will do the job.

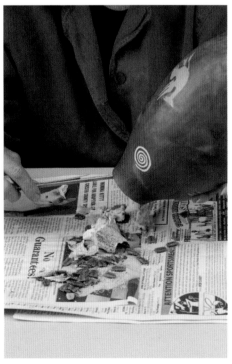

Dump the seeds and scrape out with a skewer.

Sand the top smooth.

Glue the saucer onto the bottom of the gourd.

Position and let dry.

Apply trim to the top of the saucer. This is garden twine made into cord (see birdhouse).

Carefully butt the ends.

37

A single ply of twine goes in a groove on the saucer.

A couple coats of wax gives a nice sheen.

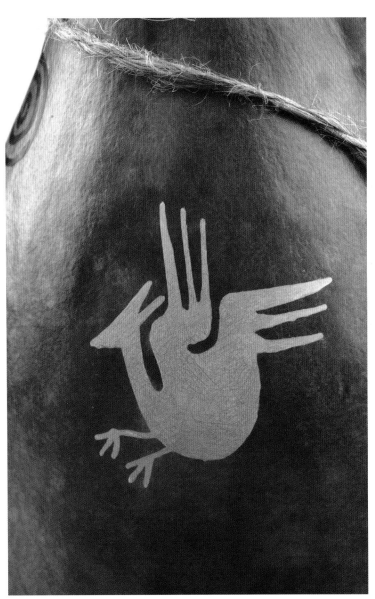

The inlays are perfectly flat and cannot be felt with the fingers.

A little necklace and it's done.

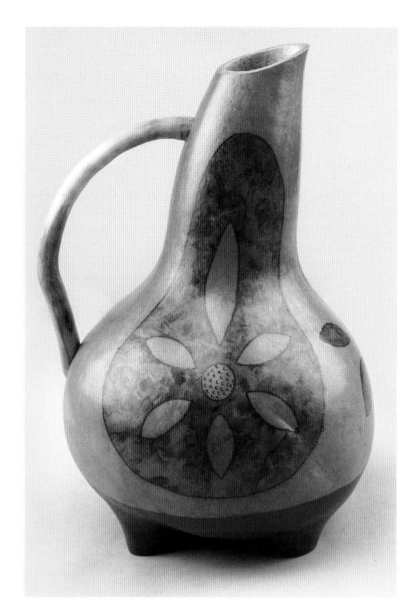

Chapter 7
Faux Burl Ewer

In this project we will introduce wood-burning combined with a simple painting technique, applied handle, and the making of feet.

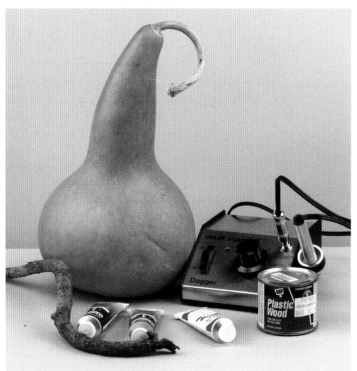

Materials: Wood burning tool, Plastic Wood, burnt sienna, burnt umber, and yellow ocher tube oils, Lazy Susan, compass, push pins, and material for handle.

Place three or four push pins (or ball pins if they are too long) where you want the feet to be. Move them around to achieve the best balance and up and down for correct tilt. They will act as an armature for the Plastic Wood and a stop for sanding. Any extra holes made are easily filled with the Plastic Wood.

This gourd sits crooked so I'll add some feet to straighten it up.

Pins placed to balance the gourd.

Begin packing in the Plastic Wood.

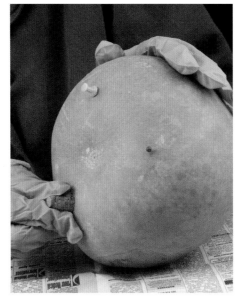

Fingers make the best shapers; but wear gloves, Plastic Wood is sticky!

Put as much on as seems reasonable. Let dry.

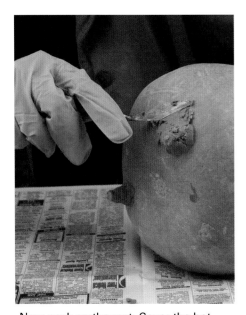

Now pack on the rest. Cover the bottom of the pins as well.

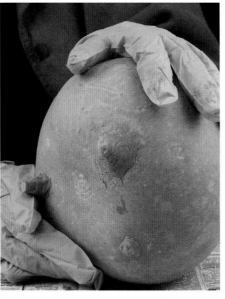

Foot complete. Repeat for the other feet. Let dry.

I want these feet nice and fat. These are dry and ready to sand.

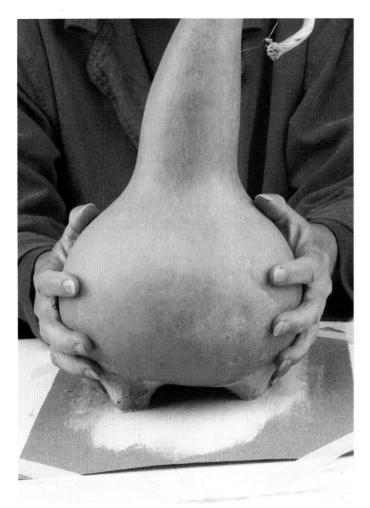

Sand the feet on a piece of sandpaper taped to a flat surface.

Stop when the pins start to show through.

Shape the feet with a rasp, rotary tool with drum sanding attachment or sandpaper.

Feet done.

All of these are good possibilities for a handle: a) curved part of another gourd; b) forked stick; c) curved stick.

I'll use this curved debarked stick for this one. Mark the holes to insert the handle.

Puncture the center with the ball cutter in the rotary tool and carefully nip off the edges. You want a careful fit here.

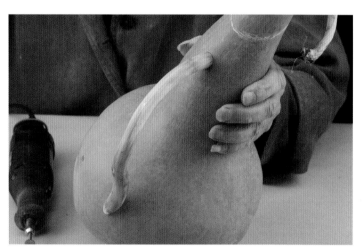

A good fit. Repeat for the other end.

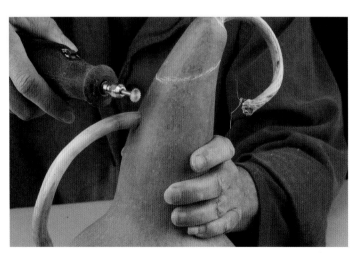

Mark the neck for cutting and use the tool of your choice. I'm using a cutting wheel in the rotary tool.

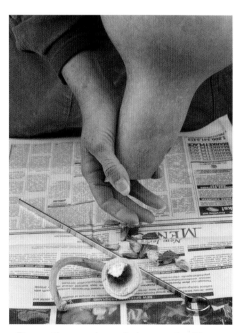

Dump the seeds and clean out with a skewer.

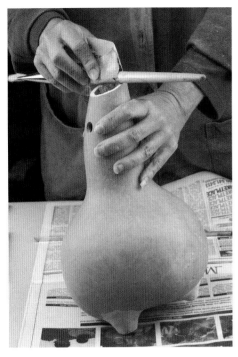

Sand the neck smooth.

Put the gourd on the Lazy Susan and mark the paint line with the compass.

Tape the line.

Paint the bottom with craft paint.

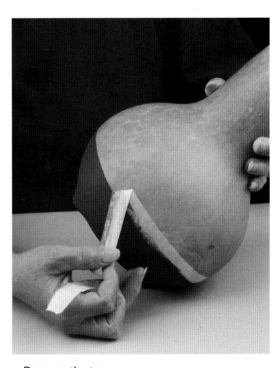

Remove the tape.

43

With the handle temporarily in place, make a shape with a piece of chalk. Chalk allows more freedom and it wipes right off if you don't like it.

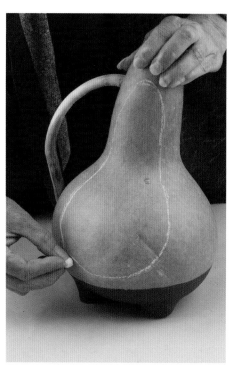

Do both sides, then go over the line with a pencil and wipe away the chalk.

Transfer the flower into each shape and one flower on the front.

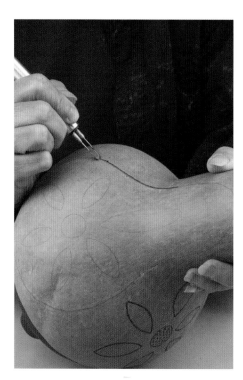

With the transfers complete, burn the line, moving slowly and evenly. Use a low temperature so as not to burn through the gourd wall. This tip is rounded and makes a thicker line.

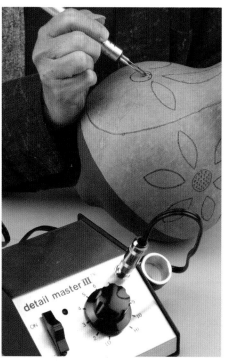

Burn all the lines and add some dots in the flower centers. Remove pencil lines with window cleaner.

Burning complete.

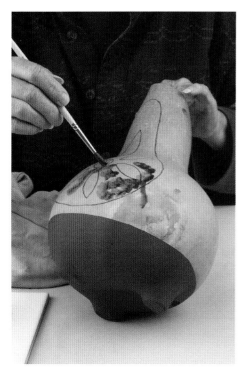

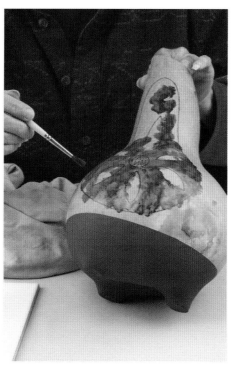

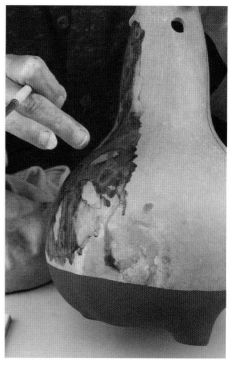

Apply the paint by adding LOTS of turpentine to the three colors and dabbling them on the surface.

Just let it all puddle.

Dipping your finger in the paint adds a nice texture.

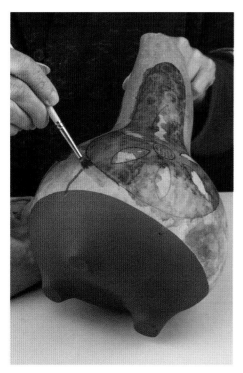

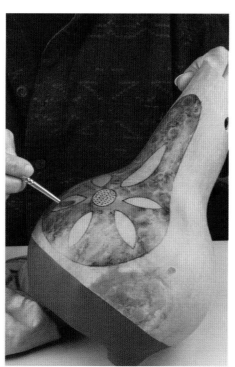

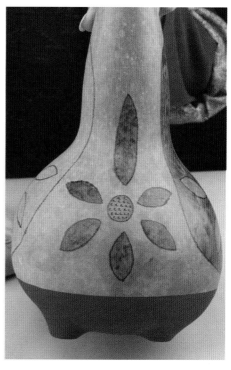

Remove the slop-overs by dipping the brush in the turpentine, wiping it on a rag, and picking the paint off.

Clean out all the petals.

On the front paint the inside of the petals. Let dry thoroughly.

Glue in the handle. If the
fit is "gappy," apply a trim.
Apply a topcoat. I used
Zar satin polyurethane.

The finished ewer.

46

Chapter 8
Scarecrow Roly-poly

This project utilizes burning and acrylic glazes to make a figure, or in this case a roly-poly. You need a bird bottle gourd with a round bottom in order to do this. If your gourd is flat, a figure that doesn't roll may be made.

Materials list: Wood burning tool, plaster of Paris, toilet paper tube, acrylics or craft paints, water-based varnish or acrylic medium such as Liquitex™.

This gourd has a nice round bottom.

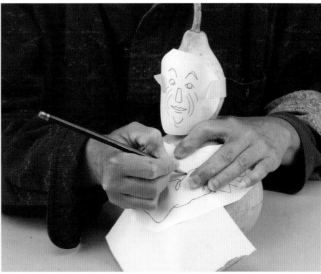

Transfer the drawings of the hands and face onto the

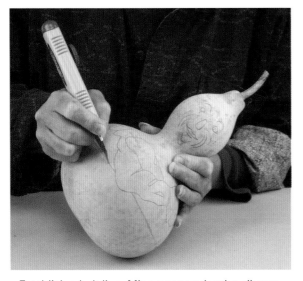

Establish a belt line. Mine goes under the elbows. This is where the cut will be made.

The thinnest possible cut line is needed so the two halves of the gourd will go back together properly. Cut with the knife along the beltline and under the elbows.

Open the gourd and clean it out.

Dust the bottom out. A roly-poly needs to be center weighted to work properly. Hold a toilet paper tube in the center of the bottom and pour in a little plaster of Paris. Hold the tube a few moments until the plaster begins to set up and it won't run out the bottom. Let dry.

Weight dried.

Tape the gourd together and check the balance. The gourd should tip from one side ...

and back again without falling over. Plaster may be added or removed to achieve good balance.

Run a bead of glue around the rim.

Tape together and let dry.

Complete the drawing. There is a floppy hat with a rope around the face, ruffle around the neck with a rope, and the coat drapes under the belt. Completed drawing, front ...

and back.

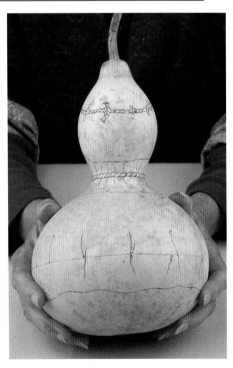

Burn the line. This pointy tip gives a fine line. Clean up the pencil marks with window cleaner when you're done.

Burning complete, front ...

and back.

Mix your acrylics with the medium and begin the painting. Keep it transparent so as not to lose the line – you can always go back over it. The hat is black.

The coat is green.

The "pants" are solid brown.

Add details. Brown eyes and eyebrows...

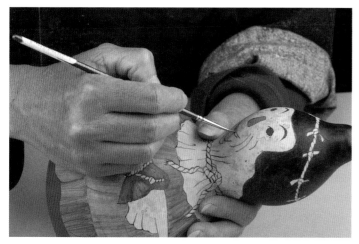

mauve brown nose and lips...

light gray gloves and ropes.

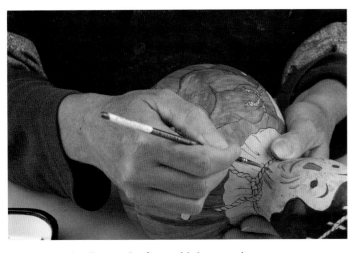

Add some shading to the face with brown glaze...

and darker greens to the folds of the coat.

Front painting complete.

Back painting complete.

By soaking the stem in warm water I was able to split it into "straw."

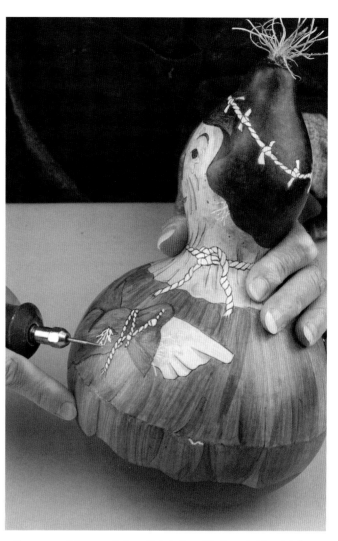

You can add some "straw" details with the etching bit in the rotary tool.

Glue some twine over the cut line to make a belt.

Scarecrow roly-poly complete.

Sources

Dick Blick
Art and craft supplies of all kinds at discount prices. Catalog or online.
PO Box 1267
Galesburg, IL 61402-1267
800-828-4548

Eli Smucker
Home-grown gourds, leather dyes and tools.
317 Springville Road
Kinzers, PA 17535
717-354-6118

Gallery

Vase, batik and acrylics

Iris Bowl, watercolors

Bowl and Votive

Birdhouses

Kalimbas

Gourd, cedar shingle

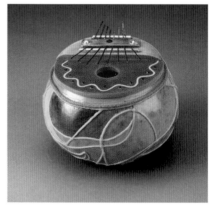

Glazes, applied string

Wood burning, oil glazes

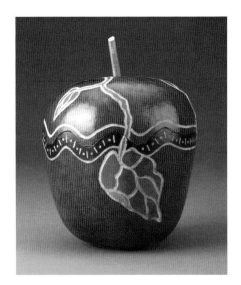

Apple box

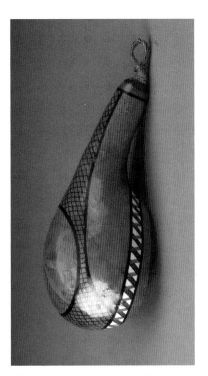

Winter walk, oils

Dipper, pen and ink, acrylics

Nut Case, shellac,
leather hinges

Seed holder, burning, inlay

What a Rack!, Gourd top, natural
stick

Roly poly

Bobble head snapping turtle

Bird House patterns

Japanese Maple

White Oak

Maple

Red Oak

Elm

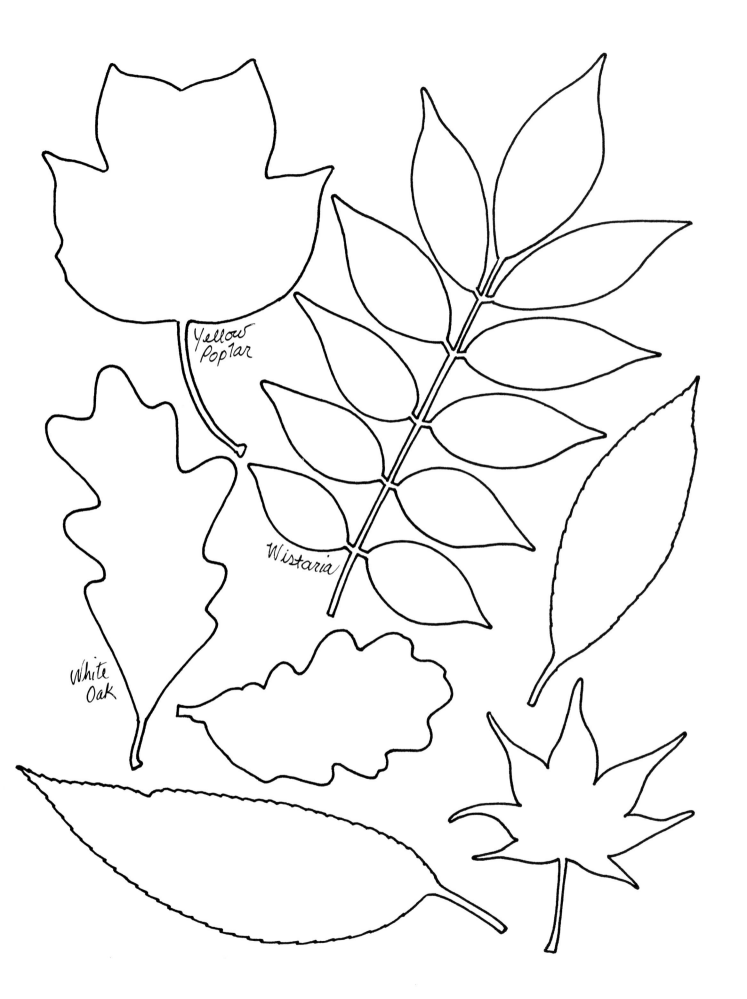

Yellow Poplar

Wistaria

White Oak

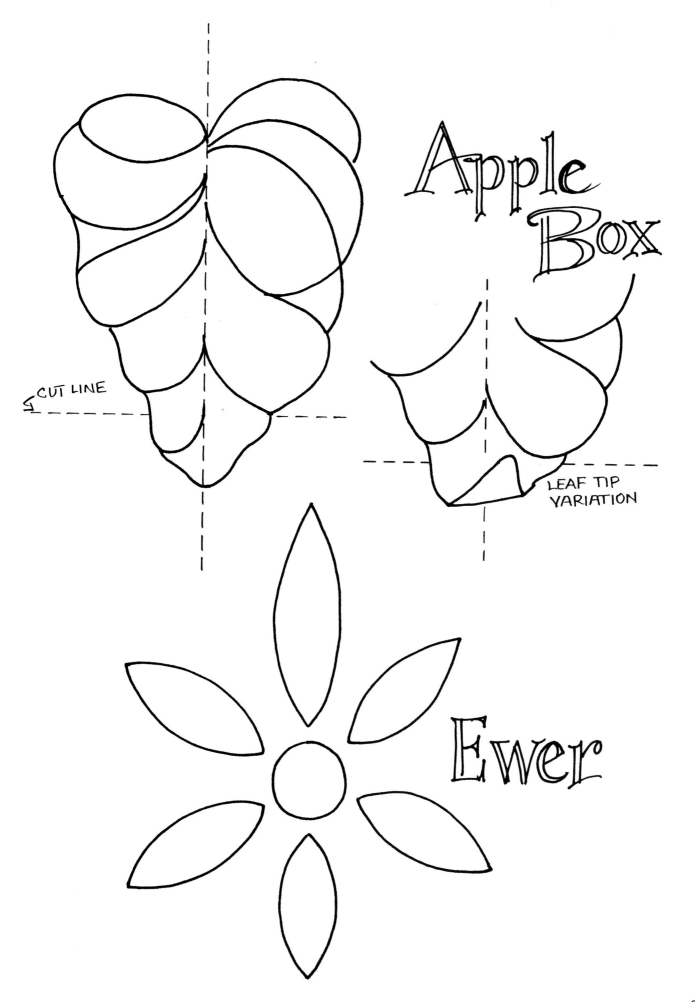

CUT LINE

Apple
Box

LEAF TIP
VARIATION

Ewer

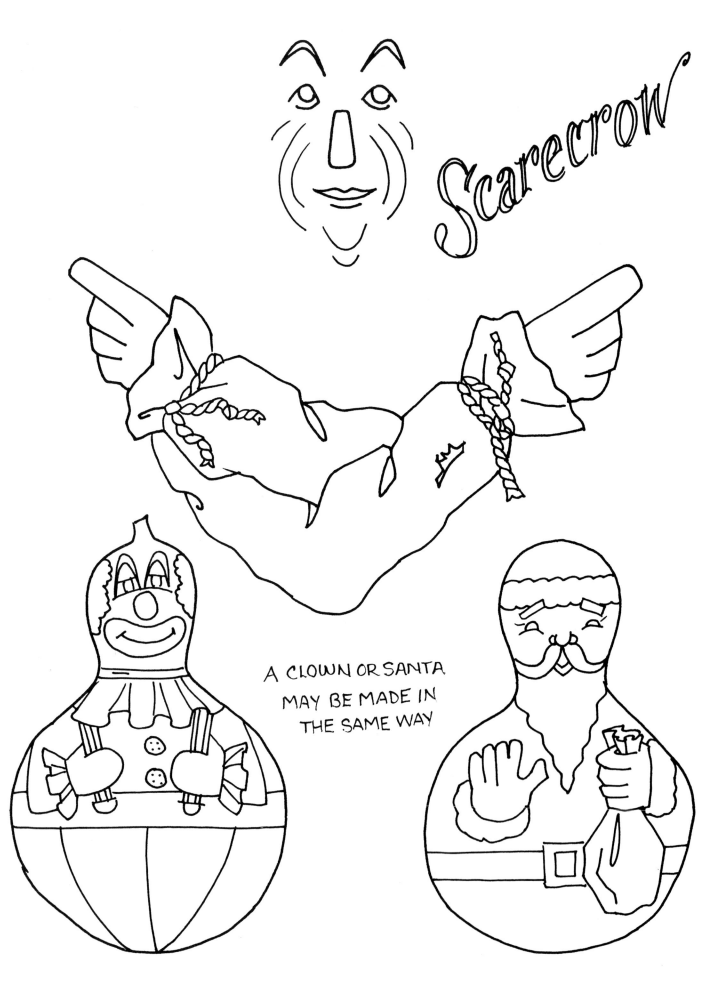

Scarecrow

A CLOWN OR SANTA
MAY BE MADE IN
THE SAME WAY